Rosemary Shaw has changed since having her craniotomy. She feels like a more complete individual after her operation.

She realizes now how terrible things were and kriss cross, young lady as she would call herself, has a great deal to say thanks to Fred for being found.

Fred is the name she gave her tumour and made an honest effort not to allow things to get her down and now because of Fred if she needs help, she will ask. At the point when she has a medical issue, the old Rosemary would make an honest effort to disregard it, however, this new normal of being well is her mentality.

While out for a walk, to the shops, it is clear she is in trouble as legs are not moving, she waves her hands up high. This is kriss cross lady.

She can speak much better for herself despite the fact she is introvert.

Rosemary Shaw

LIFE AFTER A CRANIOTOMY OPERATION

AUSTIN MACAULEY PUBLISHERS™
LONDON • CAMBRIDGE • NEW YORK • SHARJAH

Copyright © Rosemary Shaw 2024

The right of Rosemary Shaw to be identified as author of this work has been asserted by the author in accordance with sections 77 and 78 of the Copyright, Designs and Patents Act 1988.

All rights reserved. No part of this publication may be reproduced, stored in a retrieval system, or transmitted in any form or by any means, electronic, mechanical, photocopying, recording, or otherwise, without the prior permission of the publishers.

Any person who commits any unauthorised act in relation to this publication may be liable to criminal prosecution and civil claims for damages.

All of the events in this memoir are true to the best of author's memory. The views expressed in this memoir are solely those of the author.

A CIP catalogue record for this title is available from the British Library.

ISBN 9781035833023 (Paperback)
ISBN 9781035833030 (ePub e-book)

www.austinmacauley.com

First Published 2024
Austin Macauley Publishers Ltd®
1 Canada Square
Canary Wharf
London
E14 5AA

Firstly, I would like to thank the medical community for giving me back something which I could easily have lost.

Secondly, thank you to my friends, family and work colleagues who kept me going at work by talking to me, smiling and encouraging me when things looked bad.

Lastly, I would like to thank Brain as they helped me immensely.

Table of Contents

Prologue	11
Oxford	13
Where Do You Get Help?	15
When Do You Have to React to Your Changing Circumstances?	17
Craniotomy	20
Living Your Best Life; Is That a True Saying?	21
Media	23
I Am Not Healthy	26
Diagnosis	29
What Does Benign Mean?	31
Operation Day	36
The Team in Neurosurgery Has Done My Operation	37
Going Back to Work	39
Walkabout at the Hospital	43
Time	44
The New Normal	47

What Does a Craniotomy Patient Expect from Their Operation?	**49**
Peace and Quiet	**53**
Work of a Perfectionist	**55**
Recovery Is a Bitch!	**60**
What Is Recovery?	**63**
What Is Fair?	**68**
Workplace	**70**
Sound	**72**
Speech and Language Therapy	**74**
The Five Senses That I Feel Were Always Important to Me Are…	**77**
Touch	**79**
Singing	**84**
Can Anyone Ever Fix Me?	**87**
The Food Festival	**90**
Anxiety	**94**
Stereotactic Radiotherapy	**97**
Zapping Time	**99**
Why Does Work Matter So Much to Me?	**100**
What Is Time?	**102**
Visiting the Doctors	**103**
Running Out of Time	**104**

Future 106

Epilogue 108

Prologue

Fred has arrived and is causing trouble.

Who is Fred?

He is the name of my tumour, but it is called a meningioma grade 1 and is benign.

I have written this book to say thank you to the people who operated on my head. I have a quality of life and can do the things that matter to me. I still have difficulties but before the operation, left was right, right was left, and eyes were closing. I was jumping on hearing loud noises and my legs were unable to walk. Double vision and speech problems all occurred, and a whole host of other things: Speech was unclear and words hard to find I knew the words but not able to pronounce them. Looking for things proved difficult even though they were in plain view like my glasses and remembering where I put items.

What does the word meningioma mean?

The word meningioma is used to describe tumours that grow in the brain and need to be looked at by Consultants in Neurosurgery. My tumour is slow growing and forms in the meninges (a thin layer of tissue that covers and protects the brain and spinal cord).

These tumours if not found can cause life-threating problems.

I was diagnosed in 2015 and gobsmacked to say the least but always had a few individual problems going on beforehand. This meant I spent a lot of time going up and down to the doctors and saying something is wrong and not sure what is wrong.

I was put on a watch and wait list after my tumour was found, as this tumour is not operated on unless it is giving problems.

This operation would have happened sooner but due to my blood pressure problems, I had to wait, and other things.

Oxford

The hospital is like talking about Cambridge to me and so I think of it as posh. Its lovely and when I was on the ward looking out the windows, I saw neat allotments and green spaces, churches, schools a park. Lots of people biking and a good cross section of diverse cultures and people. In the building as I walked about, I noticed beautiful paintings and corridors that had information about its heritage written on picture frames and posters. While driving to Oxford I passed lots of villages and streams and new and old buildings. A train station that connected the outside cities was also hidden in this tranquil place and nearby a lovely pub selling fish and chips. Narrow lanes that made sure you stopped or else it there would be an accident and a few bridges that had stood the test of time and fields with crops growing and of course cows, sheep, and horses. At times we passed slow moving tractors laden with hay.

All hospitals know their field of expertise, but Oxford has a department that concentrates on Neuroscience as a lot of hospitals changed to become places of excellence. So, wherever you are in England there are places you can go to be seen by experts.

My GP at my surgery had sent me with a referral letter and this made it clear l needed to be seen. As I waited in A& E other people were suffering and in distress, but all l kept feeling was will, they believe I am not well. Please do not send me home.

I arrived at the emergency department with my family and was seen by the triage staff but all the time I kept wishing. Please do not send me home. As I was becoming increasingly scared as my symptoms were coming and going. I needed help.

Relief at being placed on a ward in a bed after several hours wait was great and the family left in the early hour of the morning only to return as speech was not clear to the nurse who was asking questions of me.

Where Do You Get Help?

Firstly NHS, then a website called BRIAN specially designed to support those with brain tumours and their families. Neuro Nurse who is based in your local hospital and gives advice over the phone. My GP Surgery who can ask the hospital where you are being treated for advice.

The John Radcliffe Hospital where I had surgery, GOOGLE – SELF HELP GROUPS in your area as it can be a comfort to talk to those in a similar situation. Lastly BOOKS other INTERNET SEARCH ENGINES can help also.

There are many instances you know things are wrong and you need to react to them, but you hope rest will make things better. For me it was increasingly clear that l was not getting better, so I went to doctors and things progressed from there. I work in the post office, and it is a place where people are helpful, and this is not always the case.

One day while doing overtime, I pushed a York with parcels to the designated position. But I could not remember how I got there. So, I said to my shift manager can I go home. She said yes and enquired if I will be all right. This was the start of me going rapidly downhill. Several other things had happened like looking at the noticeboard and seeing my name in double vision. Most morning I would awake with a headache and vomiting, breathing problems would also affect me.

I live 20 minutes from the hospital, and it is easy to pop in. But 1 do not. I do not like hospitals and after a few experiences my impression of them has changed. I do not want to make a fuss. I do not want to be in there if nothing is wrong and feel like a fool. So, l wait even when I know I need to go I head for my own bed.

Not everyone wants help and not everyone is willing to except it.

1. Pride
2. Stubborn
3. Overconfident
4. Stupid
5. Scared

When Do You Have to React to Your Changing Circumstances?

Several times I knew something was wrong but when I woke up the next day, I would say things look better. I was not a good employee anymore at work and was always bringing sick notes to work. My job felt that it was always on the line to me, and I would not have blamed my employer for sacking me. I still work for the post office, and this enabled me to keep independent and have a positive outcome. So, I was able to pay my bills and keep my home.

Past Present and Future

Who is going to do my operation?

Neurosurgeons

What is the operation?

Stereotactic Craniotomy

When will I be ready?

When the team say I am, because it must be planned

Why do I need to have this operation?

I need this operation as things are becoming increasing difficult and chances of a good outcome do not look good to me.

Life is for living but at this moment I am existing.

.

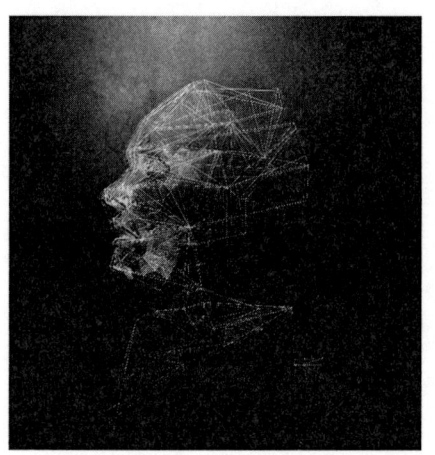

Craniotomy

The brain is the most important thing that a human being has and without one you die. A heart can be transplanted, and you have a chance, but a brain, no.

Are you ever afraid of the dark? Well, I am never afraid of the dark, as nothing can hurt you unless you give up, remain confident and try to work out what is going on.

But I was very scared.

1. Will I be me.
2. Will I be able to talk?
3. Will I be able to understand?
4. Will I know my family?
5. Will I survive.
6. Will I ever walk?
7. Will I be a wife?
8. Will I ever be the mother that I was before? Caring, loving, reasonable,
9. Will I ever work again?
10. How will I support myself in my family?

Living Your Best Life; Is That a True Saying?

There are no guarantees in life but when asked the obvious I quietly said to myself I am having this operation before my family could even discuss it with the consultant.

I knew this was my only chance.

What are some of my symptoms?

I cannot walk. I cannot speak. I feel I am losing all the things that we as humans take for granted. Writing and reading is part of your education, but I am losing this ability. The sun would shine outside in the garden, and as it hit my head, I started going downhill and my eyes closed. Then my walking slowed down. The most confusing thing is I knew it was not right and I was in no pain. But think about, really, it is time to get help.

It took me a year to read a book after my operation, not because I did not know the words. But I could not concentrate all the time. I love to read and am quite a quick reader so after my operation I picked up a book I brought with me. I could read it and understand. I also brought in photos of family members without their names. The hospital paperwork recommend you brought things to familiarise yourself. This was a test to see if l recognised my family members, but later as the weeks and months progressed at home things changed.

You open your eyes in the morning and look through the window outside. I have a garden and there is a tree and flowers it is quite neat, and I enjoy my home as its where I have lived for 22 years. It is the one place l feel safe but when I come home its feel new and not my home. I cannot remember how things work and everything has a newness about it.

The people around me are my neighbour's and some of them I call a friend and have a good relationship with them.

Most days I go to work at the post office, and it is my place of work, and where I have been for several years. But lately I am not sure what is going on. I am distracted and, on the internet, looking at other people with tumour problems. Will I be the same?

While watching television I always pick up the threads that something medical is about to happened. I start to listen and relax and then the word tumour.

Media

I love listening to the radio and come across a play called the Coma Patient on Radio 4. I listen to it so many times l can tell the scenarios before they happen. So, reading books and newspapers and watching television I have a good understanding of what is about to happen. The thread that something medical and life changing will happen, is happening and all to me.

What Does the Word Tumour Mean?

The definition in the dictionary says it is a mass growing on or in the body.

So, what does it mean to me? Sadly, I am having issues.

I am not doing well and for once in my life some of the help yourself ideas on the notice board at work and in books, pamphlets in the hospital and my surgery are being picked up. I am reading books and articles and asking questions.

The internet becomes my new best friend as things I feel unable to ask, I just ask.

These questions come in repeated waves but are they the right questions, who knows I just want to be alive and want answers.

What Is Healthy?

Healthy is you are well do not need to have an operation. It means you visit the doctors for normal aliments, and you try to be as honest as you can. But when they say something is wrong, well, you must be open about everything that is going on.

You ask questions?

But really, I want things to be back to normal.

The definition of the word normal as defined in the dictionary is typical, usual, regular.

I Am Not Healthy

When I go to work, I am in fear of my legs not working and my eyes shutting down and I seem confused at times. My legs have stopped working properly, and my eyes close like a light switch being switched on and off. When this happens, my husband comes to pick me up from work. As he arrives, I am also aware that feet are not working. So, I am helped into the car. We pull up on the driveway and I hobble in and then there is the urgency to go to the loo. But I am not in control, barely able to rush upstairs, and then it is into bed.

If You Need Help, Ring This Number?

First Class is on the work noticeboard, I ring it as I want answers a lady is on the other end of the phone. I do not know her, and she does not know me. I talk about my problem which is my forthcoming operation and diagnosis and leaves me tearful. Do I need more help, no, well yes, but where to start? She talked and l listened and as the conversation progressed, I felt better.

I cried a lot because I was scared because the world around does not always help people even when it is clear they need help. You are constantly asked to prove you are not well. Why?

If a doctor says you are ill and others agree why is this not the standard as, all I could think of was how much more time would I need off work.

How would we pay our bills and keep our home?

What if we lose our home?

What will happen?

There is a line in every agreement regarding money that reminds you if you do not pay you are in danger of losing your home.

Before my operation it was like been stuck on a roundabout as blood pressure was unstable and I had various tests to do which included wearing an ambulatory monitor for blood pressure for a couple of days. My sick leave was dwindling but when you are ill you do not have a choice how much time you have off. The condition dictates your days and what you can do.

Diagnosis

When told my diagnosis by the consultant at my local hospital, I asked if he was looking on the right brain. He replied yes. So, it is all true yes, but I just need to confirm it with Oxford.

I left the hospital and passed a shop in the hospital selling sweets and bought a packet of fruit pastilles and gobbled them noting the taste, size and colour and never thought to share with anyone. As when I was younger the colour green had a special saying, and it came into my head.

Would You Share Your Fruit Pastilles?

When I met with consultants, I still did not take my situation on board and reading it in black and white only made me wonder if things are so bad. In one of my consultations was a 3D model that the consultant showed of my head. It was interesting and as I looked at it, the thoughts that came into my head, is this the shape of my nose and eyes, my brain and the outline of my head is so clear.

I have seen lots of sci fi films but the technology of using a tool to turn it this way and that is so quick. So, a good picture of my head from any angle that needs to be defined is shown me.

The keyword in this consultation is its benign and I am not going to die.

What Does Benign Mean?

The definition of benign is not malignant.

Which means a good chance to survive?

Does any of this make sense, or have I missed the conversation?

Life expectancy was five years is that what he said, and things will be better, better for me.

Or is that what I want to hear?

Life Skills

I love to read, dance, listen to music, play sport and listening to stories on the radio, the world interests me and the television. The person I am means I can cook, garden, knit, sew, and make things. I feel confident in most things and will always try to do my best.

What Is This Person Like Now?

I walk a straight line to my back door because l knows exactly where my clothesline is, and I can feel the clothes drying on the line. Post it notes reminded me what to do before answering my front door. I become frightened of noise and groups of people seem loud. My family would do the shopping in the supermarket as I became disturbed by the chatting of people. So, I just sat in the car and waited while they shopped for things for our home. There are times my breathing is off, and l am anxious and the thought of been left on my own is frightening. I would clock watch if I could, but just get on with it as I know my family are at work and I must get on with my day.

What If This Is It for the Rest of My Life?

Well, this and more happen to me. But the real story is, in fact, I am alive.

The bad days, I was in pain and tablets barely took away the pain. Blood pressure was going up and down vomiting and headaches were the normal.

When I had a good day, it was just like the old me always busy and for example winning most games of badminton and going for bike rides. I would also visit the cinema and meeting up for lunch with friends.

While playing badminton I noticed that I am having trouble holding my racket and doing smashes, decorating is hard as my hands have become weak. I drop things suddenly. I even spilled paint on a new rug I had bought my daughter. The can just dropped.

In a world where healthy means you can work nothing worries you more than your ability to do a job and take care of yourself.

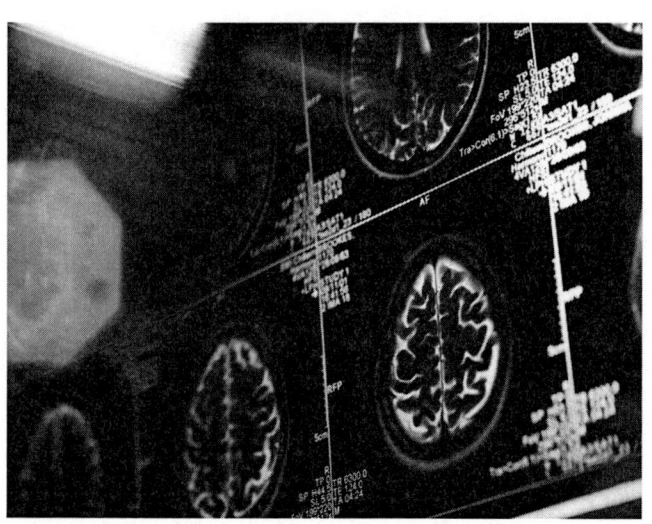

Operation Day

So, it is the day of the operation, and this has been agreed before I went up to the ward. It is 1 June 2017 and my son's birthday is 1 June. An extremely easy one to remember but I do not as I start taking a certain medication. I am away with the birds and not there. Second time around and a quicker response to this steroid medication, it is so quick but this time I was at least in the hospital and doctors could manage my condition.

Do I know you? Are you making sense to me? Forgetful and drifting like a boat at sea without a mast. Barely able to write and confused. The television is on, but it has a fault, so I use it with ease no input required but after the operation I cannot work it.

I am in a new room and things are working but l cannot work them without help. Remembering the days of the weeks I cheat as the lunch menu comes around it has the next day name.

The Team in Neurosurgery Has Done My Operation

What are my days really like?

The good days are I can wake up from sleep and spread my bed while at home, but a bad day is I have no energy to spread the bed. Then I start looking at my home and completing the jobs. The phone would ring, and I would answer it and just say my name and put it down. I have breakfast and awake, and the cup of tea is stone cold when I stir again. What a to-do.

I remember the television on in the background and me not really paying attention. Then I start to do some gardening and need a cushion. I am so tired, but weeds are growing and nothing looking nice, just over, so the Chelsea Chop is taking place. The grass needed mowing, but I get out of breath trying to use the electric mower.

There is another man unwell on my street and we talk about our aliments which helps me to put in perspective my own. Sometimes you feel like things are happening only to you but by sharing things it feels better talking.

I would like to attend family celebrations, but I barely leave the house and the sofa becomes my new best friend. My thoughts are confused and remembering things is frustrating.

At a family celebration it is all well set up and a bar on hand to serve drinks. When the guests arrive, one shouts out hello Auntie in the car park. I respond with a blank expression. It is my niece, but I do not recognise her, and she looks at me and says Auntie has forgotten me.

If I had to explain this occurrence it would be you see the person, but you struggle to remember everything like when you fall and hurt yourself it takes time to heal.

Then the music starts, and it plays in the background and lovely food is served. I move from table to table and have a feeling of not fitting in and end up sitting in a corner. Granddad comes over to me and talks but I am far away with the birds. I drift in and out as he talks. Family and friends are dancing but I barely move I do not feel the music and do not join in.

I also go to a gig in my town, and it is nice to be out, and I dance for an hour and then slowly I get tired. The main event arrives at twelve, but I have already left the building.

Later that year a nephew gets married, and I am much better I cannot stop dancing and have an enjoyable time.

Going Back to Work

On my return to work, for two weeks I walked early in the morning to get my legs working better. But I still grew tired at work. The old shift proved long and hard to do, so I asked to reduce my hours, this was the right choice for me. Some people cope; well, but I did not.

I felt so tired and tried different things like going to bed early, a hot chocolate before bed. Reading and turning off anything that might stimulate me. Kindle, mobile, Tv, radio. I could not fall asleep. There were times I speak so fast and then so slow and then it was normal.

A colleague at work mention trying something to give me energy at he was a marathon runner. But I tried so many different things none really worked. I just needed to take my time.

Sometimes you are so eager to go back to work, you make things worse. So, if you need to have more time say you are not well enough yet to the doctor or your workplace.

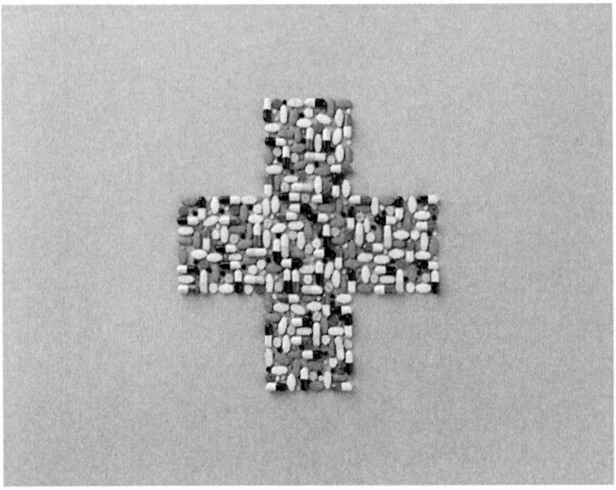

Medication

Some steroids do a fantastic job but if you get too much, it may cause a problem. I know they can help as my wrist was giving trouble and a consultant gave me an injection. This helped my wrist heal, but I still reacted. So, taking a steroid that had given me trouble in the past was not easy, but I wanted my head sorted. I needed help and quickly.

As I am now well, when asked to take that medication I had previously, I refused and was offered a different one. This worked and I had no problems.

My daughter gave me this knowing look, mummy again. Yes, I said as I took the medication. I want my head sorted out. Previously, I had spent three weeks in Oxford with them getting me off this steroid.

Before the operation they sat us down in a room to discuss things. But I had already made up my mind. And told my family one question each do you hear, they looked at me and although they wanted to ask question after question. They listened and talked to the consultant, and I had the last word.

We had talked about things and my predicament was a lot worse this time. There was no point in rehashing things as it was clear I am deteriorating.

If you are on fire, you want someone to put you out quickly. Well, I am on fire, and I just want things to go back to normal.

Walkabout at the Hospital

Well, drama… that is me, something scared me; voices that were chatting and saying I am all alone. No family. No connections, my life was not my own. You will do this, and you will give me everything that is yours and your family. Like back when people had no choices. We will get you to do this and give us everything. We always have choices. I love my life. I love my family and know I am part of them and packed my bags and left the hospital, who talks like that anyway it is the 21st century. But that feeling of dread never left me so what happened next was expected.

Time

I cannot tell you what time it was, but once dressed and packed I stood in the staff car park waiting for my husband. I know it was early in the morning and it was light. He was not waiting for me in the car and never had any idea I had not rung him to come and pick me up. When told by staff he was upset but controlled himself. My family had a few choice words and chatted at me not too me. I even contemplated getting on a bus, where too?

Lost But Never Faraway

So, I was found in the staff carpark by a fairy godmother in the shape of a nurse. She must have remembered me and coaxed me inside to the hospital. I listened and she calmly made me feel safe, she was with some colleagues just coming into work. That woman calmed me down and brought me back onto the ward and I never said thank you. But I am grateful she took care of me. Some people have the kind of face you can trust, and their tone is one you can hear; therefore, they are in the caring field. Long hours and rude patients and complex decisions that must be made are the order of their days.

Tracker Time

What is that noise? as a bracelet went on my wrist, everywhere I went, off the ward noise. It was loud and piercing and made sure I stayed put and safe until I had my operation.

I was not the best patient by far the worst, rude, difficult, and opinionated and did not listen to my family, nurse, or doctors. The people at the hospital got a patient that could not listen. But they looked after me, cared for me, and did their best.

The New Normal

I still wanted to go for walks early in the morning all alone and, well, wonder woman I was not. Can you a imagine a patient just had her operation walking at the front of the hospital? Intent on carrying on her daily routine?

I love to go for a walk and run first thing in the morning and its usual before anyone is out of bed. Fresh air makes me feel good and has always been a part of me. In my life, I have played tennis, netball and tried karate, Zumba, aerobics, Tai Chi, joined gyms and run for pleasure and charity.

It Is not easy to look after a patient but that is why I can honestly say, repeatedly thank you for keeping me safe.

Strange dreams even now affect me and remind me of that night in the hospital and I do not like them. I do not watch violence and bad story lines. I like old movies and things that make me laugh and are family.

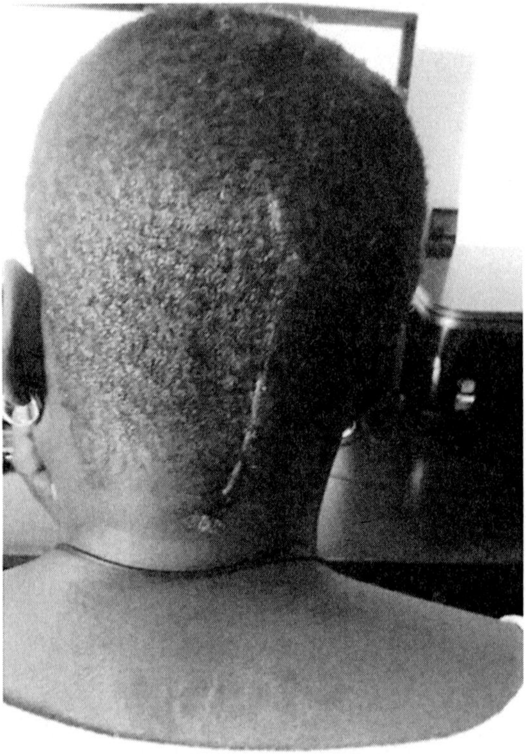

What Does a Craniotomy Patient Expect from Their Operation?

There are times I wonder do all craniotomy patients experience so much and then I realise it is all down to the individual who is having the operation. The skill of the surgeon and the staff who take care of you is not in doubt. But no two people are the same. We all want to be the same as before but is it feasible. I know now how lucky I am to be alive and able to do most things and the old me and new are one person.

1 June 2017 – Operation Day

I have had my operation and 13 hours of excellent work, a team of neurosurgeons working on my head, and everything done to keep me alive. My head was cut open with an incision and the stereotactic craniotomy has been performed. I never felt a thing and was out cold. But here comes more drama…

To Say It's Musketeer Time Would Be Awful but Rose...

What is this on my head?
What is going on?
I am awful, where to begin.
Take this off my head?
What is this inside of me?

It is not good. There are times like a dream I can remember doing all this and feel what a total disaster.

But that hospital still looked after me even after the first reaction which I had so I was able to have my operation.

On that occasion my reflection in the mirror was strange as I saw the top half of my body and the shape was different. Watching a movie was at accelerated speed. The Eurovision song contest was on the television, and noise and strobe lights I had to turn the television off. My feet seem large and the weight gain, well, I understand legs that rub more now. My daughter contacted the hospital on my behalf to ask questions about my medication.

Its auto pilot and nothing is going to be the same again but I have had my operation

Definition of medication reaction

The catheter line is out, the cannula is out, and the drain for my head is gone. Suddenly there is cutting, a window is open.

This window does not open wide safety is on all windows in a hospital.

The whatever it is called at the back of head is touched until a nurse says, 'Please leave it alone, Rosemary.'

It's removed.

When someone says your full name, it's usually to grab your attention.

But this woman is not really listening.

It is me. My god, do I remember it and honestly I feel shocked, embarrassed and would like to hide away but as an adult, I must take some responsibility.

When I come home from hospital and meet up with a colleague for a chat, I tell her all that's happened to me, and I feel this overwhelming shock and embarrassment. But it is good to say it aloud so I can move on with my life. It is not good to cover up things that happen.

Better in than out, an idiom goes, and I think that is right.

Peace and Quiet

Later when I am home and can remember things, I think of a place that is so quiet no noise. Everyone dressed in white and in a cubicle, with a blue glow. I felt safe, why do they take you away from this place. Is this place real I do not know. But I wish it were, peaceful and calm like water moves in ripples and no sound.

I also remember looking into the mirror and saying where are you Rose? When I was back on the ward. I did not know who was looking back at me in the mirror. I rang my home and said I am awake, when are you coming to visit me. When the family come, I got all upset if they had their phones on. It was like they are loud but not even on. Everything took time. And I do mean everything.

Many years ago, I had a dealt with catheter while I worked in care. A client had one that was blocked. When we arrived, he was crying sat in the chair and not saying much. We done care and the next time we visited he was not home he was suffering from a UTI but his face I will never forget. I too suffered from a blocked catheter and will never forget the pain. It was worse than giving birth to me.

Self-harmed

I cannot cover it up as self-harming time had happened.

Yes, me again. For me it is still confusing as the scars are in sharp vision, was it before or after my operation. But a scar on my chest and wrist will tell the tale of a woman not in control. I survived my operation and am ashamed l behaved so bad.

The brain is like a an eggshell so I believe when its operated on time helps it mend and heal. If you crack an egg and then try to put the shell back is everything the same. No, but if you have a layer which you can build around the shell it slowly merges back together.

But so happy to be alive but after my surgery I still do not fully comprehend what has happen. This makes me a challenging patient and one that is unpredictable.

Some things do not agree with me like certain tablets so if I remember I say no and have it on my records as feeling out of control is not an experience I want ever to repeat again.

I hope I do remember but this new me does not always get things right.

Work of a Perfectionist

I have a line at the back of my head that I call a zip and when it healed it was flat and neat the sewing was expert. Medical programs where surgeons practice sewing up skin on objects do not reflect its harder than you think. I have no bumps, and no keloids and it only gives me itching.

The itching on my scar line has helped me understand when things are wrong as pain can indicate something is wrong and the skin looking sore or swollen.

I had my stitches taken out of the back of my head by my local surgery and my recovery proceeds at normal pace.

Diva in the House

My daughter, husband, and son all get a taste of the new me after I return home and, well, if they could run, I am sure they would have. So, you can imagine what staff and doctors got at the hospital. I could not tell you if this was just me, but I can tell you they did best look after me.

I said things, was abrupt, and made decisions in a matter-of-fact way. I remember seeing my pots and pans in the kitchen. A few scratches here, and well, I thought they were new. But in my head unrepeatable phrases popped up.

As I walked into my kitchen, I knew it looked nice but could not remember how to access the cupboards. The oven timer proved too much, and a timer was purchased. I brought two. The family laughed but it helped me get confident with my kitchen again.

I even forgot to eat and even though I reheated things in the microwave I would find them the next day.

The tumble dryer was suffering the same fate, sometimes I remembered to completely take out the clothes. Other times the next day I found them inside the tumble dryer.

Family

My family come to visit, and a nephew sees me for the first time, and he is saying to my daughter Auntie is not well. This is true. My hands are in the air, and I lean like the leaning Tower of Pisa. I am distracted and although I am listening, miss bits of the conversation.

But this does improve in time.

What Dates and Times Do You Always Remember?

People's birthday or anniversary were either too late or too early or forgotten. If there was a family get together, I was never sure if I was going to be well. Sometimes I was just too nervous to leave the house. When the phone rang, I would be polite say my name and sometimes hang up. The early days were not too good.

Appointments That Can Be Overlooked

The hospital would ring, and I would be competent then forget everything and not tell my family. One time a nice young man on the phone got the diva, sadly. He was asking to speak to my daughter so he could inform her of my forthcoming appointment.

Friends would invite me to meet them, but it took time to trust myself and leave the house. This overwhelming feeling of De je Vue would happen, and I wanted to be safe.

My doctor's surgery wrote down my next appointment time which I am incredibly grateful for as you have guessed it without the mobile or a piece of paper, I can be forgetful.

The mobile I could use but I would look for icons and there were in front of me, and I would not see them. My list of contacts disappeared and then slowly I would return them.

I always say family first everyone after and tried to keep to that until I was ready to deal with everything.

Recovery Is a Bitch!

It takes weeks, months, and years to grow into the kind of person that is stable and does not feel out of their depth. That is why I always say without friends, family, and work colleagues the doctors and the hospital I would not be the person I am now.

When I went to an appointment with a consultant, I never knew what to ask. Suddenly I cannot remember what to ask. I feel out of my depth. Many people have a written list, I have none. So, I listen and then something wonderful happened to me my consultant said, sit down and proceeded to communicate to me and my husband. He explained to my husband and well, it was better him than me as I was still not there. Only eager to return to work.

Ups and downs and spending more time going to the doctors and the hospital and ringing the Neuro Nurse. All I want to hear is I am well.

What is well?

Well, **stable** is a start to me; it means no more surgery just MRI. But guess what; I even got scared of having MRI as what is a consultant looking for?

If like me you have had a head operation, questions are always coming,

What does a surgeon see?

Is it possible to replicate and repair the damage exactly, even if it is already deteriorating?

How do they know what to cut?

Does a brain work better than before as the joining of neural connections is different?

Recovery

I always thought getting better after an operation needed care, love, time, patience but after neurosurgery, my head is more understanding of people and their situations because care comes at a cost; if no advice is given or real help, we are all in trouble.

What Is Recovery?

At this point I have been through more unpleasant issues.

Its Saturday and the weekly shopping trip have begun but I do not leave the car. After a lot of expeditions, I find people a bit too loud, and I still have-not found my comfort zone. So as the weeks progress, I am shopping, and it looks like I know how to do everything.

Big mistake, as when I look around, I am by myself and wanting to pay for a few things l picked up.

What is tap? I cannot remember how to pay for things and ask an assistant who looks at me like what?

Well, I leave the things on the side and walk out of the supermarket. My family have finished loading the car. Then I say, do not ever leave me in there like that again. Do you understand. Panic stricken. Then my daughter says, Sorry mummy.

Recovery Takes Time

It is a mine field for me after my operation. There are times I am so confident; butter would melt in my mouth. Other times guess work.

A nice old man was talking to my daughter while I waited in the background. Who is this man? I am looking at him. But I do not know him. But he is an old family friend and l have no recollection of him.

While browsing in my local supermarket to pick up a few things and a workmate from my workplace said hello. Who is this woman my family said? I said Post Office, but I did not know her name.

At home I remember exercises taught at school and at sessions I went to for to keep fit. So, I try to get fit. You see the left side of me is not working so well and my head does turn but slowly and not at full rotation.

My garden is my gym and my phone with my earphones plugged in, music. I also walk to my local park and do a walk run, thing. I get to know a few people walking their dogs, but one man gets a special hug as we talk about our lives. This man has his own problems, but he always walks his lovely dog Holly, and she is beautiful.

At Home, Learning Things All Over Again

One morning after my husband goes to work it is time for the photo albums, but all the photos are taken out. I do not know this one. Who is this person? And suddenly there is a pile of photos. In it a woman and her daughter playing in the garden. I look. It must be someone else.

It is me and my daughter. I do not recognise myself or her.

I see a photograph of my mum and I stare at it; I know the dress, but do I know the person. Then, I remember I brought that dress for my mum. Silly, but all true.

This is what I mean when you get a head operation are you looking for everything just like before. Well, if you are, that is not fair.

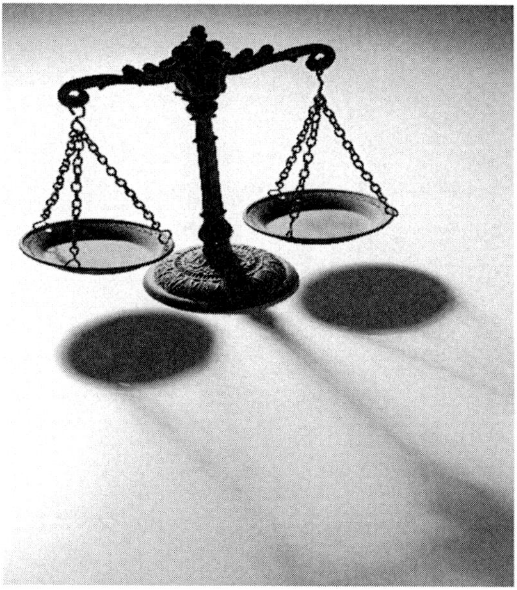

What Is Fair?

Fair is you are alive and starting to do things for yourself and taking control of your life and the operation has been a success as you are not dead.

At Oxford during one of my appointments I noticed people in my environment. The way people walked and stood and their peculiar actions. Some people moved like I do now, and others had no real control of their bodies. But one young man stood out to me. He was in a wheelchair with a halo on his head. The wheelchair moved by him controlling it. His mother walked beside him. She made no attempt to take control. On the other side of the lift stood a nurse seemingly watching them heading for the children ward.

This truly to me was amazing as when you think you have nothing take a good look around.

TRY to keep going and TRY to remember you have nothing to lose.

Everything that you thought you lost comes back and extraordinary, interesting things occur.

I wish I could say life was easy, but it is not.

My job has given me back my independence and life is looking rosy.

Workplace

Well, it is the day to go to work and I am excited to say the least, and as I walk in everything looks clean. Amazingly the ceiling is so bright, did a feather duster go up there and clean. The picture in reception looks new. But no, everything is as it should be. My friend repeats the old line, which it has always been there and reality kicks in.

I sit with a group of women, and they are work colleagues, but I call them friends. They helped me when things were going up and down. There are times that someone would show me how to do things. They would also ask me question and involve me. This proved beneficial as I had to use my voice.

At work people say hello to me and this proved important as l had to think of this person's name. Names are hard to remember so badges helped, and even now I get them wrong. Not pleasant for the person but when I get it right Wow.

The first day at school is always hard but if you know someone you feel better. If I told you I remember my school days this would be the truth as before it was a bit of a blur. While visiting old places I remember the streets and roads we took to arrive at our destination. In the old days we used maps, using a satnav was not easy for me as technology can be confusing to use.

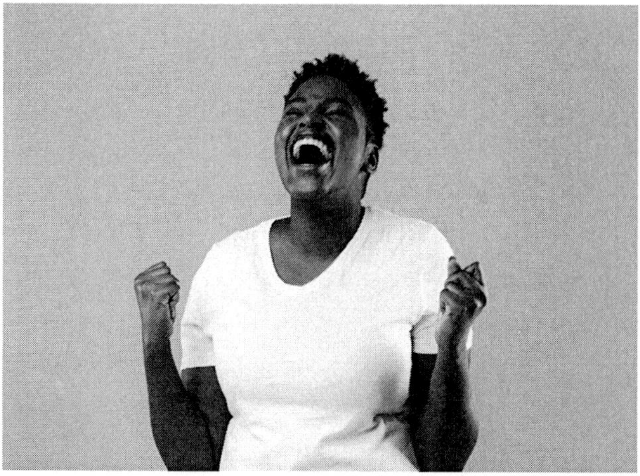

Sound

One day while at work there is an awful sound, its strained and hoarse and out of time. Oh no, shit, shit it is me. My vocal cords are all over the place and it comes and goes even now.

I even went to A&E and said I need to speak to someone as my pronunciation of some words was causing great distress to me and I could not keep saying to myself that a woman my age cannot speak good English. I also kept saying a phrase which now again still comes out. So as time goes on, I say speech and feet are a problem. The head can be like eggs frying on high heat. It does get better, but I never know if it is gone for good like my speech and feet.

I Am Born and Bred

Well, to me this means I was born in this country and this is my home. Whenever I go on holiday, I look forward to coming home to England as I love the place where I was born and have grown up.

Recap sounded like Recrap not good. The letter W, A was a nightmare and people's names. My pronunciation leaves a lot for people to understand. Sometimes I always remember things and others they are just not there and I must ask repeatedly, the same question. At work I took to looking at the badges at first and then it improved.

So, after my operation on my head my speech is gobble goop at times. Things that I learnt to do on a computer need to be relearned and I am lucky enough to do an English and Math's course that is free with my workplace. I play games on my mobile like spelling, math's, chess and do crossword puzzles. At first, I am rubbish but in time things improve. My doctor even refers me to SALT.

Speech and Language Therapy

I had an appointment, and they reassure me with my husband I am doing okay. Lots of information is given to us to read. Some of it l have already implemented into my daily activities and on the positive when my daughter worked for the NHS, she asked people's advice about what she could do that might help my recovery.

Ups and Downs

The worst thing is I sacked myself from work. Love the answer machine. I wish I could explain but it is a total nightmare.

Think of the head like a pumping heart and, all the things that the heart does, well, the brain is the heart, and you need to give it time.

But on the positive I saw a man I worked with just before we broke up for the Xmas holidays 2021. We greeted each other and I knew him. The last time we met I was in the land of nod. Who are you again? Blank patches of memory but just remember they all come back. Plus, more.

I have a new picture every day until things settle down and always you hope to make the right decisions. But perception of certain things cannot always be trusted and when you look at a picture what do you see?

A phrase I like to use is thinking creatively and to me it means you look at things repeatedly and from different angles. It means you must keep thinking beyond four corners and above and below and when you see an object analyse: box, square, triangle.

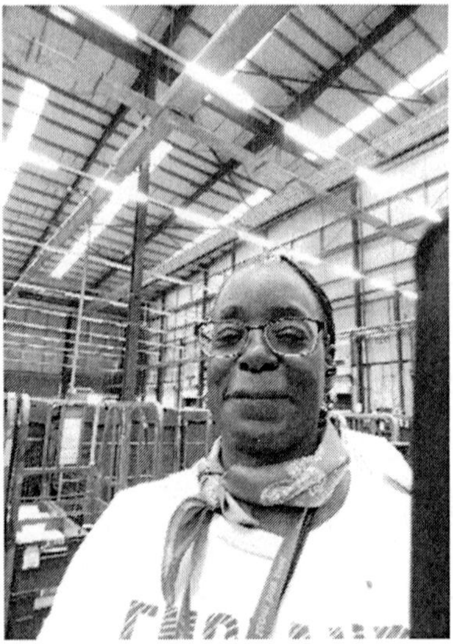

The Five Senses That I Feel Were Always Important to Me Are...

- Smell
- Touch
- Taste
- Sound
- Sight

Smell

I could not smell anything for a long time and the Covid 19 situation helped me. Some of the things that people talked about happened to me. At the time you feel like a nincompoop as why can you not smell things.

I went through a phase where everybody at work smelt the same. Why. Then suddenly you smell different scents on individuals. I would say nose is working. Smelling bacon as I walked or ran pass people houses. Knowing the smell from flowers. Opening a pint of milk and being able to acknowledge it is okay to use.

While visiting my sister in hospital who was having treatment for metastatic breast cancer. I met another person who had been operated at Oxford. It was refreshing to hear someone express the things that were happening to me. I cannot smell anything. I cannot taste anything. What is going on? You feel like you are going up and down. When is it going to stop, and when will you be normal?

Touch

I love the feel of certain things and noticed my hands would feel things more. Not sure why as never paid attention to it before. I still have hands in the air and moving at the sound of music. Not always able to stop it. But not embarrassed by been different. I call it the new normal. When you touch a petal of a flower do you feel it. The texture is it smooth, rough, delicate, and easy to dissolve. Well, after the head operation I feel things more.

There are times my head felt like a pin cushion, and I compared it to frying eggs on heat. Sometimes the cold whipped through me like a gust of wind. Things are much better now but wrapped like a mummy or boxer before a fight nothing out of the ordinary for me.

Kissing is a pleasure and to say I felt differently would not be a lie. My husband kissed me, and it was like the first time when we met. Butterflies and a sense of more please. You see not all things are the same but for me a second chance at falling in love, remembering the first time. Yes, I experience all that and more.

Emotions

I never knew what happy meant but the smallest things make me happy and cheerful. I feel good. Reading, looking at flowers, photos, walking, watching a movie. They are hazard at times. There are times I could cry and not understand why. When my sister died, and it hurt, the pain and my sobs almost stopped me from doing daily tasks. The routine of work helped me to keep moving forward, as I was not in control. Feeling a loss is never easy but when it is your baby sister everything is put in focus like a partner, child, friend, relative, pet. Their part in your life was important.

Remembering family times with her and with her own family and friends gave me the confidence to keep going.

Taste

I love the taste of some foods and fish and chips is my favourite even when I was going to school. I find I will happily go into my workplace early so l can have it. When I returned home from hospital, I could not stand anything spicy or too hot.

My poor husband puts spice on everything while l am the bland cook. It does not worry me as I enjoyed the food while l was in hospital. I noticed the colour and presentation of the food. The tastes were interesting on my palette. I ate food that I am not sure l use to like, and the flavours and sensation were lovely, but as l am not vegan it did not matter.

But a phrase I stopped saying was nose is working, because I could taste things, I could smell things.

Sound

I love music but went through a spell when l could not move to it or experience any pleasure from it. I seem unable to react. But it all came back to me in a distinct way that makes me different or unique I do not know. l can dance and love to be in the garden trying to stretch and make my muscles work out. As I know how lucky I am to be able to do what I do.

If I can remember to turn the music down, it is good but loud or soft it affects me. Music reminds me to use my senses and feel the emotion behind the sound. This means I am able to move and feel like I am getting better. Just like an audio book you react to the story line and the voice, tone, accent and then you know whether it is an informative read or not.

What Do You Hear When Music Is Played?

I hear the pitch and I listen for the musical instruments. The sound of the person singing and whether its appealing to me. Does it make me feel happy or sad?

Sound

Tempo, speed

Bass, Treble, Alto, Soprano,

Instruments

Drums, Guitar, Piano, Violin. Flute, Oboe, Triangles, Bells, Trumpets

Singing

When I came home from hospital l sang late at night to sportify and swayed in my bed. Even at the hospital I am remembering singing hymns and making more noise that most patients. They never once said shut up Rose.

Another patient would walk up and down the ward saying something. The words were always repetitive, but he expressed himself, and it was comforting.

I experience sounds of voices talking in the hospital which frighten me greatly and still experience episodes of this, not sure why. But l am a believer nothing can hurt you and when and if you need help you will be given the right help.

Sight

I wear glasses and with them my vision is perfection, without them 1 can see but not things faraway. Imagine you are in hospital and not everything is clear to you. I am on medication, and it has changed my perception of things around me. I cannot always work things out. Also, my glasses got destroyed in hospital by me.

After my head operation I went for a walk and looked at my environment. The shrubs were in bloom and every green in view could be seen. They had an intensely bright and vivid colours. To say chloroform, had highlighted my senses would not be untrue as my vison of my scenery was beautiful.

I am amazed at my surroundings and feel lucky to see life in all its splendour and feel a profound sense of happy and lucky to be alive.

Events That Should Have Highlighted That It Was Time for Me to Seek Help

The time I knew was going to have this head operation was when. One Sunday morning I asked my husband to take me for a walk. There is an alley way which is a short cut to another street. As we leave the house left is right and right is left.

The hands and feet cannot form a straight line. Robotic and out of step l give in again to the awful truth. Things are not what they are supposed to be.

There was a time I felt my left foot dragging and I still ignored it. Why?

I took extra aspirin but did not go to hospital immediately, as I did not want to waste anyone's time. I love listening to the Radio 4 and another play reminded me what to do if you think you are having a stroke. Act FAST.

I did everything but go on about my situation.

Can Anyone Ever Fix Me?

It is now I realise l might not make it back to being me. I am a mess. Everything is changing and l might get lost in this real situation.

What makes me, me?

What enables us to think and do all the things that make us human?

Do you ever pray?

Well, if there is something wrong?

Hell, I am first on the list.

Please this, please that, and even the Bible will come out.

But I am frightened, scared, and well, walking tall. I am not. So, when it is your turn do not feel bad. We all want to live.

When Is a Problem Not to Be Ignored?

I visited the doctors as my issues were increasing becoming a problem and most of the time l felt like a complete fool. I rang so often; speed dial was not off the list but what is the matter with you now.

This is how l felt as each time the doctors were calling Oxford, and Oxford was trying to sort things out.

One day as I walked to the doctors for my appointment, and I had just been met by my nephew in the car park, things took a turn for the worst. I could not keep walking to his mother's house. As he pushed me from behind and encouraged me to walk. Pacing was only able and after few steps I could no longer walk. The sun had hit my head and closing had started again.

Auntie come on, walk and that frantic look of a teenager with the high-pitched voice. People walked by us and looked, and all the time l should have said back to the doctors please. But it was too late. So, we ambled along to his mother's house. Well, she has a staircase like the Tower of London.

Usually, I fly up them like wonder woman. But not today. I hover with my hands in the air and my nephew takes out his phone to ring his mum who is at work in London. She responds and takes the train home after talking to her boss, that her sister is in distress.

By which time my other nephew has turned up in his car and lifted me up and put me in the car. I am shown dignity. Except Rose, really feels her life is changing at an alarming rate.

I am the one who is supposed to be caring for the child, but on this occasion, he is looking after Auntie.

You see these events only clarify to me that I needed help, but I do not go to the hospital. I go to bed and rest and then my daughter arrives and husband. They look at me and ask the relevant questions, but as l am fed up with the system and what to do, I just get on with it.

The Food Festival

Before my operation

The Food Festival came to my town with lots of different food and chefs cooking. It was a lovely sunny day, and we were looking forward to it as a family activity we could all enjoy. As l sat in the crowd watching Levi Roots, cook, my head would bob up and down. Stupid is an unkind word but still l did not go to hospital, and I was ten minutes away. My head was switching on and off like a light switch. This was becoming regular, and you guessed it still I did not go to my local hospital. You see I had visited so much I felt like l was a waste of time and got fed of feeling like what is wrong with this woman now?

Why Do I Not Do Something?

I even go to work like, no I am not ringing in sick again. Me and that answerphone.

As I arrive for the Work Time Learning, which is a weekly event, and take a seat in the pod. The manager greets us and begins. At the end of the meeting, she tells my friend politely to do something. I am picked up by my husband and taken home. You see still becoming afraid of a head operation and all that it could mean. Still suffering from high blood pressure and waiting for a date that has already moved once.

What a to do. I like my job; I like my workplace. But most of all there are a lot of jobs out there. But this one I love and get paid for, and the people are all from diverse cultures and express themselves and I know I am part of the workforce.

Visiting My Sister

One day I went to visit my sister as she was having a serious operation and the need to see her was the only thing that mattered. We drove down to London and incidents on the way made sure I should have gone home.

But onward I go, at a service station l saw a manager and he looked at me. I said hello and followed my daughter to the ladies. This was a spectacle holding on to her coat tails. But some of my situations are unbelievable but sadly all true.

There are always times, places, and events you look back on and say this should be it. But for me it was not.

(So, if you feel unwell, keep going and ask for help)

My recovery after my head operation has more ups and downs

This is a reminder that even when you think you are well, you are not

I come home from hospital and to say I feel good is no understatement, but the diva is still trying to be in command. My son is asked to take me for a walk up the road. But l as we walk, I am falling asleep the feet are hard to lift and tiredness hits me like someone is keeping me down. As we make to the front door, he says I am not doing that again. Do you hear? But as usual, I am not really listening.

Anxiety

Flooding is a normal occurrence in England due to global warming, now. But I make more noise when my husband drives through water. There is a stream that has become a river and the water has burst its banks. Both sides of this lane, road are converged, and it is just water and deep. Not even a puddle.

The car at least is high enough from the ground for the water not to come in. But what are you doing? Driving. The noise is horrendous, but he just keeps going. This is while driving to an appointment in Oxford.

Crete

I am in the family hire car and my daughter is driving up a steep hill. You see Crete is a lovely place but stop the car. I will walk. And breathing and saying really, really. No, no. My nephew is holding my hand and it is squeezed like a hard piece of wood. This wood is something he has carried from the time his mother died.

Auntie, Auntie it is okay, my daughter shouts out I will stop in a minute. My husband says continue driving to my daughter.

It Is Raining Cats and Dogs

Even when going to work I can experience an overwhelming dread of water, water, everywhere if there has been flooding. So, if you need help keep going back. It took a long time before I took tablets properly. But they helped me.

So back to doctors again and asking for help. You see I get the tablets but do not take them if any reaction is unpleasant. Still frighten of reacting to medication.

Who is this woman?

Why does she not listen?

As a child I read Oliver Twist the expression more, well I say to myself more why?

The woman in me is suddenly a child, I do not want too. Why? Why? Me.

Stereotactic Radiotherapy

The last bit of tumour needs to be treated and is near my brain stem and I agree to have it dealt with. Fred has siblings and well they are still causing problems its **Stereotactic Radiotherapy** now. There is one more piece of the tumour to get as the neurosurgeons could not get it all. But strangely, I am not afraid. In fact, let's get this done and concentrate just on getting better.

Hospice

While visiting my sister at the hospice I met staff and saw other patients in passing. It is a lovely place to be in and its quiet and the surrounding are pleasant. We are allowed to visit more often than the hospital and can sit with my sister and understand the time is coming soon to say goodbye. Her son spends loads of time with her and this means he is happy.

A man brought a dog in called Jesse it was cute and friendly and had amazing eyes that looked right through you. Jesse visited all the patients, and it was lovely to see that some pets are in the hospice and touching that dog made you feel good.

As I walked back to my sister's room that dog came running to me and stood looking at me. I bent down and petted Jesse and he looked up at me. Although he cannot speak something passed between us and I said I know, I know I have not finished yet. Those eyes went through me. Warm and encouraging and a sense of calm came over me. He ran back to his master and a smile occurred.

If I had to describe this time, I would say pets have a sixth sense and we do not recognise it enough.

Zapping Time

So, the blast from the past and future hits the head actual it is called **Stereotactic Radiotherapy**. A special mask was worn, and it fitted tight like a pair of gloves one size to small. The man that made it, made me laugh and put me at my ease. The procedure started and I was turned and positioned with expert precision.

I enjoyed this more and did everything that was asked of me. In the months that followed I lost a patch of hair, but it grew back in time. I also did not take too much time off work. The usual problems occurred but not as bad and although I am still going up and down it is not so frequent.

I answer questions on BRIAN daily, and my family call it my New Dear Diary; I like having somewhere to list my current situation.

Why Does Work Matter So Much to Me?

I mention work often, but this is the one place you are seen as a person. You are not a set of problems. It is up to you to prove you are capable. If you need help its always there, and you do not even have to ask. The managers in your place of work are paying attention whether you think they are or not.

Workplace

One day as I arrived in reception was a black woman called Mary Seacole in a cardboard cut-out. I remembered doing a talk on her in college. She was a nurse about the same time as Florence Nightingale during the Crimean war. The NHS is something we take for granted. But when you are sick all, I want is care. But the right care for me. I think back to my ideals while studying at college and things learnt as l have grown to become the person l am now. So always remember reading things on a work notice boards or in a book, the brain does find a way to recall them, and the stimulation can come from your environment.

What Is Time?

Well, have you ever heard the expression time is running out? This I said a lot of. As I helped care for my sister, I tried my best to fit in my own life and work. My sister had been diagnosed with metastatic breast cancer and was dying. She is old school, does not tell you anything, will not discuss anything. Her business is hers and no one else and you must apply everything to get information. When you do this, that is all I am saying she replies. Private, careful and strong, nothing passes her lips until she is ready.

Visiting the Doctors

My sister said I can go with her to the doctors, but here are the rules. No talking and I do not need to hear your opinion. I broke this rule often then she said no coming in just wait outside. So, I was relegated and learnt a painful lesson. I am not the patient and the patient my sister needs to be heard.

Running Out of Time

One weekend, me, my sister and daughter have blood tests; we all feel unusually sick. But my sister is the only one that comes back to say something is wrong. She deteriorates at an alarming speed and getting over the first operation, I am well going up and down. She finally admits something is very wrong and we all do what we can to make her comfortable.

There are many movies that make you wish for the unbelievable but *Running Out of Time* is a real movie and this one reminds me that we all wish for more time when it inevitable and death is coming.

The family and friends all did they best and she also had her friends from the church. District Nurses, Carers, Doctors, Hospital, Hospice. These all play a role in her condition as it is end of life care. Her son also becomes a good carer, and even though the terrible teens have had the better of him in the past. He turns into the young man she always wanted and the two of them share real quality time.

Memories

She is helping him revise and they are watching a Netflix shows, cooking together in the kitchen and him doing real care. He sits with her at every opportunity and talks about his outlook for his future. One day he is doing her hair, this has me laughing. She lets him style her hair. When I say there is not much on her head, but the pleasure she gets from it make her glow.

I cannot tell you why things happen but when they do, we do our best to work it out.

Future

Today, I am well and whatever happens, I am glad I had my operation. There have been other people who have died from this operation and not able to do everything they did before. But the true skill of an operation is that people are learning all the time.

Can computers talk to the brain; can it analyse your thoughts?

Can it map your brain so that everything is like a conversation from anywhere in the world?

Just Maybe

Computer technology has advanced, and this is only the beginning but like a sci-fi movie that has stood the test of time.

(Star Trek, we are boldly going where we have never been before.)

Thank you, Oxford, for giving me back my life and a second chance to keep going.

Epilogue

When I come home from hospital, I could barely turn my head, it's stiff and in the following years, I have achieved left to right movement and, although stiff at times, still able.

I can do high kicks and both legs are able then it's wobbling like I have been drinking. My posture can be off at times and running is different.

My feet still move slow and then fast but each day we keep going because after my first operation, I got back my feet. It took time but anything is possible.

My left side is weaker than my right, but I work at it even though it is slow.

I require help sometimes but am not afraid to ask, my speech can be off, and my hands still move whenever they like at times, but music is the one area they are doing exactly what I want.

I look normal but have a few issues and that is why I applied for a Blue Badge, and I use it. I also have a Brain Injury Card.

I enjoy my life and am grateful that I am alive. I have done a Tandem Sky Dive, Race for Life, and been on holiday with my family.

The Brian website has been useful to me as a search engine explaining some of my problems and others talking about their problems after a brain operation.

This book is written to say that we are all different and your experience is unique to you just like mine is to me. But we all find our own path.

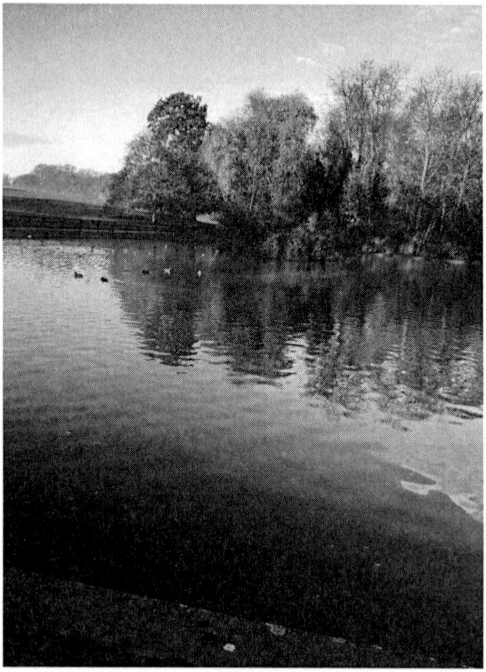